Salawat of Tremendous Blessings

Salawat of Tremendous Blessings

To Remove Black Magic, Marital Problems and Negative Energy from Your Life

From the book *Talkhīs al-Maʿarif*
by Sayyid Muḥammad ʿĀrif

Explanation by
Shaykh Muhammad Hisham Kabbani

PUBLISHED BY THE
INSTITUTE FOR SPIRITUAL AND CULTURAL ADVANCEMENT

Published and Distributed by:

Institute for Spiritual and Cultural Advancement (ISCA)
17195 Silver Parkway, #201
Fenton, MI 48430 USA
Tel: (888) 278-6624
Fax: (810) 815-0518
Email: staff@naqshbandi.org
Web: http://www.naqshbandi.org

Second Edition: October 2012
SALAWAT OF TREMENDOUS BLESSINGS (English)
ISBN: 978-1-930409-91-0

Library of Congress Cataloging-in-Publication Data

Kabbani, Muhammad Hisham.
Islamic devotional compiled by Shaykh Muhammad Hisham Kabbani. --1st ed.
p. cm. -- (salawat of tremendous blessings)
Spiritual discourses of Shaykh Muhammad Hisham Kabbani. -- 1st ed.
p. cm. -- (To remove black magic, marital problems and negative energy from your life)
ISBN: 978-1-930409-91-0 (alk. paper)
1. Naqshabandiyah. 2. Sufism. I. Title.
BP189.7.N352K327 2012
297.4'8--dc22
2010044186

PRINTED IN THE UNITED STATES OF AMERICA
15 14 13 12 11 05 06 07 08 09

Shaykh Muḥammad Hisham Kabbani is an Islamic scholar and representative of Shaykh Muḥammad Nāẓim ʿAdil al-Ḥaqqānī, global leader of the Naqshbandi-Haqqani Sufi Order. He is authorized to teach Islamic Law and to counsel seekers around the world in the science and principles of *Taṣawwuf* (Sufism), mystical Islamic teachings that date back to Prophet Muḥammad (God's Peace and Blessing be upon him).

To learn more about *Taṣawwuf*, or about moderate Islamic teachings and the results of three decades of Shaykh Kabbani's outreach to heads of state, foreign policy advisors, government ministers, print and broadcast media outlets, and leaders of other faiths and faith-based organizations, visit these websites:

www.islamicsupremecouncil.org www.eShaykh.com
www.Sufilive.com sufismcentre.co.uk

إِنَّ اللهَ وَمَلَائِكَتَهُ يُصَلُّونَ عَلَى النَّبِيِّ

يَا أَيُّهَا الَّذِينَ آمَنُوا صَلُّوا عَلَيْهِ وَسَلِّمُوا تَسْلِيمًا

Inna 'Llāha wa malā'ikatahu yuṣallūna ʿalā 'n-nabīyy,
yā ayyuha 'Lladhīna āmanū ṣallū ʿalayhi wa sallimū taslīma.

Verily, Allāh and His Angels send praise on the Prophet.
O Believers! Send blessings on him and salute him with
a worthy salutation!

(*Surat al-Aḥzāb*, 33:56)

Table of Contents

Dedication

First and foremost, this book is dedicated to the love of Prophet Muḥammad ﷺ, and to all *Ahlu 's-Sunnah wa 'l-Jama'ah* who are abiding always in the mention of Sayyīdinā Muḥammad ﷺ and his *Ṣaḥābah* ؓ with the deepest respect.

It is also dedicated to the *shuyūkh* of the eminent Golden Chain of the Naqshbandi Sufi Order, especially to Sayyīdī Shaykh Muḥammad Nāẓim 'Adil al-Ḥaqqānī ق and all his followers, and similarly, to all *mashaykh* of other esteemed *ṭarīqats* and their followers.

May Allāh ﷻ grant them a share in the rewards of this humble effort.

Foreword by Mawlana Shaykh Nazim al-Haqqani

All praise belongs to God Almighty, Who created the universe from Absolute Nothingness, Who brought the Creations into existence and illuminated them with His Light, adorning them with His Names and Attributes, and Who reflects them in the Mirror of His Reality. He honored His special servants by letting them behold the splendor of His Light, and manifested to them His abiding Presence by raising them to an exalted station!

Praise be to God, Who lavished His Divine Love on the People of Ecstasy, and adorned them with His acceptance and satisfaction, and blessed those who are seeking the most distinguished path to Him. He allows whom He likes to enter His Presence and receive from His Words, which are the Origin of Origins, the Reality of Realities, the Light of Lights! Praise belongs to Him, and through this Praise, I am asking Him to open to us the doors of His Heavenly Goodness, and that our thanks to Him are scented with the perfume of the roses of His Names!

I bear witness that He is the Only One to be worshipped, and He is the Only Source of Goodness! I bear witness that His Messenger, our supporter, Sayyīdinā Muḥammad ﷺ, is His sincere and loyal servant whom He chose to be the Heart of His Divine Essence! May God bestow His blessings on His Beloved, Prophet Muḥammad ﷺ, on his noble Family ؓ and Companions ؓ, on all those who follow in his footsteps, and on all Saints and Masters of the Most Distinguished Naqshbandi Order and of all other Sufi Orders.

May God's blessings and greetings of peace be on our beloved Prophet Muḥammad ﷺ, who is a sun from the Unseen Light of the Divine Presence that came forth and outshone the light of the sun! As he perceived he informed, and as he discovered he described. With his Light, the Light of Prophecy shone forth, and the Lights of Prophets thereby appeared. You cannot find any lights more luminous than his! Who can be brighter than The One Who Shines upon All Creation? His fervor precedes all fervors, his existence preceded Absolute Nothingness, and his name preceded the Pen, because he was before all that is and he is the Master of this Creation!

His name is Muḥammad ﷺ! He is unique! His word is confirmed! His attributes are most honored! O Mankind! Wonder at his appearance, at his visions, at his greatness, at his fame, at his Light, at his purity, at his godliness, at his power, at his Reality and his Essence! He was and remains from pre-Eternity to post-Eternity. He was known before the universes and Creation. He was known in

God's Divine Presence as 'the Heart of the Essence,' which manifests itself through him.

He was the sincere servant to his Lord from that time. He was mentioned before there was a 'before,' and he will be after there is an 'after.' He is the Sign for all signs. He is the pearl of all jewels. He is the rainbow of all colors. He is connected with God Almighty, and neither is he nor can he ever be disconnected!

All knowledge is but a drop in his ocean. All centuries are but one moment in his time. He is the truth and reality of existence. He is the first in connection and the last in prophethood. He is the internal in truth and the external in knowledge.

God Almighty sent him as His Representative from His Light, and as a sincere servant for His Creation, raising him up to His Divine Presence and putting his name next to His Name. He was a Prophet when Adam عليه السلام was between water and clay!

Greetings of peace be on his Family and illustrious Companions—may God be pleased with them all—who were guided by the greatness of his deeds, the clarity of his speech, the Light of his being, and the perfection of his religion; who drank from the oceans of his good manners, his ethics and his perfect state; who, in the attainment of knowledge and truth, bathed themselves in the spring of his secrets!

For all who read it, may this booklet be an abiding source of connection to our beloved Prophet ﷺ, and may it open infinite blessings to them, purify their hearts, relieve their burdens and crush Shaytan's influence and interference in their lives.

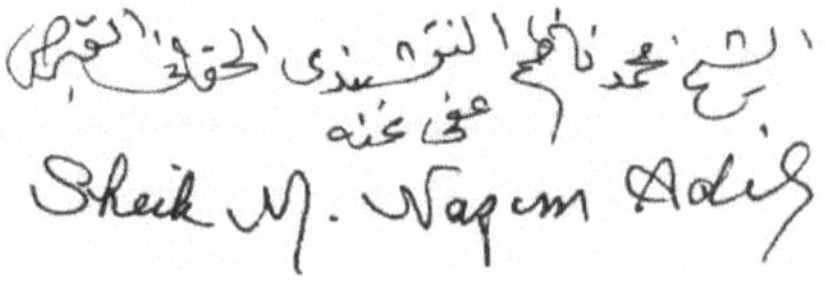

For deeper understanding of the benefits and secret powers of *ṣalawāt*, please visit www.Sufilive.com and the recent series based on Mawlana Shaykh Nazim's teachings, "The Greatness of *Ṣalawāt* on Prophet ﷺ," which features more than two dozen video lectures and transcripts[1]. To download printable files and audio recordings of the *ṣalawāt* in this book, go to http://www.sufilive.com/salawat/.

---

[1] Go to http://sufilive.com/The_Greatness_of_Salawat_on_Prophet_s_-166-s.html

Preface

The main purpose in compiling these specific *ṣalawāt* is to demonstrate the Greatness that Allāh ﷻ gave to His Beloved, Prophet Muḥammad ﷺ, and to feature the sophisticated, elegant language of past Muslim scholars and *awlīyāullāh* from around the world that is absent from modern compositions.

From North Africa, South Africa and the Subcontinent, throughout Arab countries, to the Far East and Far West, to this day the spiritual giants who composed these heart-stirring, eloquent petitions to their Lord in magnificent praise of His Beloved ﷺ are unmatched in expressing the essence of the highest form of love!

With the few exceptions being the sacred, world-renowned *Qaṣīdat al-Burdatu 'sh-Sharīfah, Qaṣīdat al-Mudarīyyah fī Madḥ Khayri 'l-Barīyyah*[2] and *Dalā'il al-Khayrāt*[3], we have not seen the likes of such transcendent, illuminating prose.

Allāh ﷻ ordered all angels—those He created in the past or present, and those whom He will create in the future—to make continuous *ṣalawāt* on the Prophet ﷺ[4], not one time only, but they praise him non-stop in every moment since they were created and they will continue until the Day of Judgment!

The greatness Allāh ﷻ has shown on His Prophet ﷺ is in the unique *ṣalawāt* of every angel, which can never be repeated! An infinite number of angels continuously recite an infinite number of *ṣalawāt* never recited before, and which will never be recited again. Their second recitation is not like their first and their fourth recitation is not like their third, as each individual *ṣalawāt* they recite comes to them as a Divine appearance!

We must never think this is too much or an exaggeration, as Allāh's ﷻ Greatness is ever higher and He can do even more than that!

---

[2]Both *qaṣa'id* were composed by the Shadhilī Shaykh Imam Muḥammad al-Būṣīrī (d. 1294), Egyptian (Moroccan Berber descent).

[3] Imam Muḥammad al-Jazuli, Morocco (d.1465).

[4] Holy Qur'an, Surat al-Aḥzāb, 33:56.

Introduction

Ṣalawāt, the invocation of praise on Prophet Muḥammad ﷺ, is a Divine Order on all believers (Holy Qur'an, 33:56). Recited since the creation of humankind, *ṣalawāt* is the means to reach higher spiritual stations and enhance one's nearness to Allāh Almighty and His Beloved Prophet ﷺ.

Ṣalawāt is known to polish the spiritual heart, allowing it to reflect heavenly attributes that are often blocked by one's preoccupation with the physical world. Specifically, frequent recitation of *ṣalawāt* builds good character and increases good desires, and diminishes bad character and removes bad desires.

This booklet is a collection of *ṣalawāt* that are known to accelerate one's spiritual advancement, which are authenticated by the Prophet ﷺ and by eminent Islamic scholars and mystics from throughout our 1500-year history.

If anyone made *ṣalawāt*, may Allāh ﷻ include a share with every worshipper in this life with the worship of the Prophet ﷺ, the *Ṣaḥābah* and all *awlīyāullāh*. If we can read these *ṣalawāts, alḥamdulillāh;* if we cannot, then say, "*Yā Rabbī*! Whatever *ṣalawāt* people have made on the Prophet ﷺ, share those rewards with us!" That is the quickest way to excel. Allāh ﷻ said, *"Ask and I will give you!"* (Holy Qur'an, 40:60) So we are asking, *"Yā Allāh*! For the sake of the *ma'ṣūmīn*, Infallible Ones, give us a share in the rewards of the worship of Your Prophets, especially that of Sayyīdinā Muḥammad ﷺ!"

As Grandshaykh 'AbdAllāh ق taught us, if you cannot recite all these *ṣalawāts*, say, *"Yā Rabbī, nawaynā mithla mā nawā Mawlanā Shaykh*. O my Lord! We are making the same intention as Mawlana Shaykh," and the same will be written for you, because it is very difficult to read them all. This is the easiest way and the way of *awlīyāullāh*.

Grandshaykh 'AbdAllāh ق showed his greatest love to the Prophet ﷺ and taught us that love, as Mawlana Shaykh Nazim ق has, may Allāh ﷻ give him long life, and to all *awlīyāullāh* and scholars quoted in this humble book. We are asking that our intention be the same as theirs, and we ask for their support as we are weak, helpless and deficient in all things and we cannot achieve anything by ourselves. We may spend our entire life trying to accomplish something, but our efforts are still that of an ant and probably not even that! Don't think your *'amal* will save you, because only their support and intercession can take us to safety!

So we ask the Prophet ﷺ and Grandshaykh ق to intercede for us and that we are granted to be with them in *dunyā* and *Ākhirah*! They can be with us, but we cannot be with them if they do not open that door and take us in, nor can we enter that realm by ourselves.

Shaykh Muḥammad Hisham Kabbani
September 2012

ℵ ℵ

Publisher's Notes

The following universally recognized symbols have been respectfully included in this work and are deeply appreciated by our readers.

ﷻ *Subḥānahu wa Taʿālā* (may His Glory be Exalted), recited after the name "Allāh" and any of the Islamic Names of God.

ﷺ *ṢallAllāhu ʿalayhi wa sallam* (God's blessings and greetings of peace be upon him), recited after the holy name of Prophet Muḥammad.

عليه السلام *ʿAlayhi 's-salām* (peace be upon him/her), recited after holy names of other Prophets, names of Prophet Muḥammad's relatives, the pure and virtuous women in Islam and angels.

رضي الله عنه *Raḍī-Allāhu ʿanhu/ʿanhā* (may God be pleased with him/her), recited after the holy names of Companions of Prophet Muḥammad.

ق *QaddasAllāhu sirrah* (may God sanctify his secret), recited after names of saints.

Transliteration

To facilitate authentic pronunciation of names, places and terms, use the following key:

Symbol	Transliteration	Symbol	Transliteration	Vowels: Long	
ء	ʼ	ط	ṭ	آ ى	ā
ب	b	ظ	ẓ	و	ū
ت	t	ع	ʻ	ي	ī
ث	th	غ	gh	Short	
ج	j	ف	f	َ	a
ح	ḥ	ق	q	ُ	u
خ	kh	ك	k	ِ	i
د	d	ل	l		
ذ	dh	م	m		
ر	r	ن	n		
ز	z	ه	h		
س	s	و	w		
ش	sh	ي	y		
ص	ṣ	ة	ah; at		
ض	ḍ	ال	al-/'l-		

Faḍā’il aṣ-Ṣalāt ‘alā ’n-Nabī

فضائل الصلاة على النبي

نقل الإمام الشعراني في كتاب حدائق الأنوار في الصلاة والسلام على النبي المختار، في الثمرات التي يجتنيها العبد بالصلاة على رسول الإسلام محمد والفوائد التي يكتسبها ويقتنيها:

1. امتثال أمر الله بالصلاة عليه.
2. موافقته سبحانه وتعالى في الصلاة عليه.
3. موافقة الملائكة في الصلاة عليه.
4. حصول عشر صلوات من الله تعالى.
5. أن يرفع له عشر درجات.
6. يكتب له عشر حسنات.
7. يمحى عنه عشر سيئات.
8. ترجى إجابة دعوته.
9. أنها سبب لشفاعته صلى الله عليه وسلم.
10. أنها سبب لغفران الذنوب وستر العيوب.
11. أنها سبب لكفاية العبد ما أهمه.
12. أنها سبب لقرب العبد منه صلى الله عليه وسلم.
13. أنها تقوم مقام الصدقة.
14. أنها سبب لقضاء الحوائج.
15. أنها سبب لصلاة الله وملائكته على المصلي.
16. أنها سبب زكاة المصلي والطهارة له.
17. أنها سبب لتبشير العبد بالجنة قبل موته.
18. أنها سبب للنجاة من أهوال يوم القيامة.
19. أنها سبب لردّه صلى الله عليه وسلم على المصلى عليه.
20. أنها سبب لتذكر ما نسيه المصلي عليه صلى الله عليه وسلم.

21. أنها سبب لطيب المجلس وأن لا يعود على أهله حسرة يوم القيامة.
22. أنها سبب لنفي الفقر عن المصلي عليه صلى الله عليه وسلم.
23. أنها تنفي عن العبد اسم البخل إذا صلى عليه عند ذكره صلى الله عليه وسلم.
24. نجاته من دعائه عليه برغم أنفه إذا تركها عند ذكره صلى الله عليه وسلم.
25. أنها تأتي بصاحبها على طريق الجنة وتخطئ بتاركها عن طريقها.
26. أنـها تنجـي من نتن المجلس الذي لا ذكر فيه اسم الله ورسوله صلى الله عليـه وسلم.
27. أنها سبب لتمام الكلام الذي ابتدئ بحمد الله والـصلاة على رسولـه صلى الله علـيه وسلم.
28. أنها سبب لفوز العبد بالجواز على الصراط.
29. أنه يخرج العبد عن الجفاء بالصلاة عليه صلى الله عليه وسلم.
30. أنها سبب لإلقاء الله تعالى الثناء الحسن على المصلي عليه صلى الله عليه وسلم بين السماء والأرض.
31. أنها سبب رحمة الله عز وجل.
32. أنها سبب البركة.
33. أنها سبب لدوام محبته صلى الله عليه وسلم وزيادتها وتضاعفها وذلك من عقود الإيمان لا يتم إلا به.
34. أنها سبب لمحبة الرسول صلى الله عليه وسلم للمصلي عليه صلى الله عليه وسلم.
35. أنها سبب لهداية العبد وحياة قلبه.
36. أنها سبب لعرض المصلي عليه صلى الله عليه وسلم وذكره عنده صلى الله عليه وسلم.
37. أنها سبب لتثبيت القدم يعني على الصراط.
38. تأدية الصلاة عليه لأقل القليل من حقه صلى الله عليه وسلم وشكر نعمة الله التي أنعم بها علينا.
39. أنها متضمنة لذكر الله وشكره ومعرفة إحسانه.
40. أن الصلاة عليه صلى الله عليه وسلم من العبد دعاء وسؤال من ربه عز وجل فتارة يدعو لنبيه صلى الله عليه وسلم وتارة لنفسه ولا يخفى ما في هذا من المزية للعبد.
41. من أعظم الثمرات وأجل الفوائد المكتسبات بالصلاة عليه صلى الله عليه وسلم انطباع صورته الكريمة في النفس.
42. أن الإكثار من الصلاة عليه صلى الله عليه وسلم يقوم مقام الشيخ المربي.

Benefits of Praising the Prophet

Imām ash-Shaʿrānī ق related in his book, "The Gardens of Light Due to the Praising and Greetings upon the Chosen Prophet," some of the fruits collected by the servant who praises the Messenger of Islam, Sayyīdinā Muḥammad ﷺ, are:

1. Obeying Allāh's Order by praising His Prophet ﷺ.
2. By praising, we are doing something Allāh ﷻ does.
3. By praising, we are doing something angels do.
4. Receiving ten *ṣalawāt* from Allāh ﷻ for one of our *ṣalawāt*s.
5. We are raised ten levels.
6. We gain ten goodnesses.
7. We are relieved of ten sins.
8. The prayer of the one praising is accepted.
9. It is the means for gaining Sayyīdinā Muḥammad's ﷺ intercession.
10. It is the means for forgiveness and the covering of our shortcomings.
11. It is the means to fend off what troubles a servant.
12. It is the means for nearness to Sayyīdinā Muḥammad ﷺ.
13. It is equal to charity.
14. It is the means by which needs are fulfilled.
15. It is the means by which the angels make *ṣalawāt* on us.
16. It is the means by which one purifies and cleans one's self.
17. It is the means by which a servant is given glad tidings of entering Heaven before he dies.
18. It is the means to avoid the trials of Judgment Day.
19. It is the means by which one receives the return greeting of Prophet ﷺ.
20. It is the means by which one remembers what he has forgotten.
21. It is the means by which a gathering is made fragrant and those attending it will not see sorrow on Judgment Day.
22. It is the means to keep away poverty from those who praise Prophet ﷺ.
23. A person who praises Prophet ﷺ can no longer be called stingy (as only a stingy person will hear his name and not praise him).
24. It is safety from being cursed for hearing his name and not praising him ﷺ.
25. *Ṣalawāt* of Prophet ﷺ guides the owner to Heaven and misguides from the path to Paradise the one who discards or leaves it.

26. Salvation from the stench of a gathering in which Allāh's Name and Prophet's name are not mentioned.
27. It perfects the words of the one who starts by praising Allāh ﷻ and His Prophet ﷺ.
28. It is the means by which a servant is granted passage over the Bridge (*Ṣirāṭ al-Mustaqīm*).
29. It removes the servant from Allāh's displeasure.
30. It is the means by which Allāh ﷻ will throw high praise between the heavens and earth on the servant who praises the Prophet.
31. It is the means by which one gains Allāh's Mercy.
32. It is the means for getting blessings.
33. It is the means by which one's love to Sayyīdinā Muḥammad ﷺ is consistent and increases, which is due to one's faith and without which it cannot be achieved.
34. It is the means by which one gains Prophet's ﷺ love.
35. It is the means for the servant's guidance and for his heart to be alive.
36. It is the means for the servant to be brought in front of Prophet ﷺ, and for his name to be mentioned in front of Prophet.
37. It is the means by which one's feet become firm on the path.
38. To make *ṣalawāt* on him is not enough to give him his right, but is a gesture of one's gratitude to him.
39. The *ṣalawāt* contains *dhikrullāh,* thanking Allāh ﷻ for letting us know of His Favors upon us.
40. The servant's *ṣalawāt* is supplication to one's Lord by which he asks for His Prophet ﷺ, and other times asks for himself, which is a beloved trait of a servant in Allāh's Presence.
41. One of the greatest fruits and grandest of benefits gained by *ṣalawāt* upon Prophet is that his honorable image is engraved on the self.
42. To praise him ﷺ excessively is like having a shaykh training you on the path.

Ṣalawāt Removes the Seventeen Bad Characters

As taught by Sufi Master Abū 'l-Ḥasan al-Kharqānī ق [5], to achieve the Station of *Tazkīyyat an-Nafs,* "Purification of the Soul," one must first eliminate the seventeen bad characteristics of the tyrannical ego, as listed below[6]. Reciting *ṣalawāt* as often as possible accelerates this elimination process.

The Seventeen Ruinous Traits *(al-Akhlāqu 'dh-Dhamīmah)*

1. Anger *(al-Ghaḍab)*
2. Love of this physical world (*Ḥubbu 'd-Dunyā*)
3. Malice, hatred (*al-Ḥiqd*)
4. Jealousy, envy (*al-Ḥasad*)
5. Vanity, conceit (*al-ʿUjb*)
6. Stinginess, miserliness (*al-Bukhl*)
7. Avarice, greed (*aṭ-Ṭamaʿ*)
8. Cowardice *(al-Jubn)*
9. Indolence, idleness (*al-Baṭalah*)
10. Arrogance, pride (*al-Kibr*)
11. Ostentation, showiness (*ar-Rīyā'*)
12. Attachment (*al-Ḥirṣ*)
13. Superiority, self-importance (*al-ʿAẓamah*)
14. Heedlessness (*al-Ghabāwah*) and Laziness (*al-Kasālah*)
15. Anxiety (*al-Hamm*)
16. Depression (*al-Ghamm*)
17. The 800 Forbidden Acts (*al-Manhīyāt*)

Ṣalawāt increases provision, removes difficulties, calms crying and difficult children; protects from demands, fire, drowning, capture, theft and fever; protects earnings; grants safety to travelers on land and sea; and, develops the mind.

[5] Persian (d. 1033). Farīd al-Dīn ʿAttār, the famous Persian poet and Sufi, called him "The King of the Kings of Sufi Masters." He was loved and admired by the great poets and philosophers of his time (i.e. Avicenna, Shah Maḥmūd of Ghazna, Abū-Saʿīd Abu 'l-Khayr, Nāṣir Khusraw).

[6] Excerpted from "The Sufi Science of Self-Realization A Guide to the Seventeen Ruinous Traits, the Ten Steps to Discipleship, and the Six Realities of the Heart." *Kabbani, Shaykh Muhammad Hisham, 2005. (Louisville, Fons Vitae, 2006), vii.*

Instructions for Reading Ṣalawāt in this Book

Grandshaykh ʿAbdAllāh al-Fā'iz ad-Dāghestānī ق often said, "The best of miracles is to be consistent (in worship)." It is far better to slowly establish religious practices that you will not stop, rather than begin a long regimen of many practices that you will not continue.

To help establish the daily habit of reading *ṣalawāt*, we recommend initially reading one *ṣalawāt* in this book each day in the prescribed number of recitations. For example, begin with "1) Ṣalawāt Nūrānīyyah (read once)", then the following day read "2) Ṣalāt al-Fāṭiḥ, (read once or ten times after ʿIshā)", and so on. In this way, readers will get the benefits of reciting *ṣalawāt* each day and will slowly build their capacity to read more without leaving this sacred practice.

Daily Recitations

1. Ṣalawāt Nūrānīyyah / Ṣalawāt al-Badawī al-Kubrā, Salutation of Īmām Aḥmad al-Badawī

2. Ṣalāt al-Fātiḥ, Salutation of the Victor

3. Ṣalāt al-Munajīyyah / Ṣalāt at-Tunjīnā, Salutation of Rescue

4. Ṣalāt al-ʿĀlī al-Qadr (For Claustrophobia), Salutation of Highest Value

5. Ṣalawāt at-Tahīyyāt, Salutation of the Prayer of Greeting

6. Jawharat al-Kamāl, Jewel of Perfection

7. Ṣalawāt Ūli 'l-ʿAzam, Salutation of Prophets Possessing Highest Purpose

8. Grandshaykh ʿAbdAllāh's Ṣalawāt

9. Ṣalawāt al-Askandarī

10. Ṣalawāt al-Bakrī

11. Ṣalawāt that Equals 100,000 Ṣalawāt

12. As-Ṣalāt al-Kāmil, The Prayer upon the Perfect One

13. Ṣalawāt Kamālīya, The Praise of Perfection

14. Ṣalāt as-Saʿadah, Praises of Happiness

15. Ṣalawāt adh-Dhātīyyah, Prayer of The Essence

16. Variation of Ṣalawāt al-Askandarī

17. Sayyid aṣ-Ṣalawāt, The Master of Salutations upon the Prophet

18. Ṣalawāt of Sayyīdinā ʿAlī

ᙏ   ᙒ

1) Ṣalawāt Nūrāniyyah/ Ṣalawāt al-Badawī al-Kubrā, Salutation of Īmām Aḥmad al-Badawī (Read 1 time daily)

In the book *Talkhīṣ al-Maʿarif* by Sayyid Muḥammad ʿĀrif, it is related that the *walī* Muḥammad al-Talmaysānī ﵁ recited *Dalā'il al-Khayrāt* 100,000 times, after which he saw the Prophet ﷺ in a dream saying to him, "O Muḥammad al-Talmaysānī! If you read Ṣalāt an-Nūrānīyyah of Āḥmad al-Badawī, it will be as if you recited *Dalā'il al-Khayrāt* 800,000 times!"

اَللَّهُمَّ صَلِّ وَسَلِّمْ وَبارِكْ عَلى سَيِّدِناَ وَمَوْلاَناَ مُحَمَّدٍ شَجَرَةِ الْاَصْلِ النُّوْرَانِيَّةِ، وَلُمْعَةِ الْقَبْضَةِ الرَّحْمَانِيَّةِ، وَأَفْضَلِ الْخَلِيْقَةِ الْاِنْسَانِيَّةِ، وَأَشْرَفِ الصُّوْرَةِ الْجُسْمَانِيَّةِ، وَمَعْدِنِ الْاَسْرَارِ الرَّبَّانِيَّةِ، وَخَزَائِنِ الْعُلُوْمِ الْاِصْطِفَائِيَّةِ، صَاحِبِ الْقَبْضَةِ الْاَصْلِيَّةِ، وَالْبَهْجَةِ السَّنِيَّةِ، وَالرُّتْبَةِ الْعَلِيَّةِ، مَنِ انْدَرَجَتِ النَّبِيُّوْنَ تَحْتَ لِوَائِهِ، فَهُمْ مِنْهُ وَاِلَيْهِ، وَصَلِّ وَسَلِّمْ وَبارِكْ عَلَيْهِ وَعَلىَ آلِهِ وَصَحْبِهِ عَدَدَ مَاخَلَقْتَ، وَرَزَقْتَ وَأَمَتَّ وَأَحْيَيْتَ اِلَى يَوْمِ تَبْعَثُ مَنْ أَفْنَيْتَ، وَسَلِّمْ تَسْلِيمًا كَثِيْرًا وَالْحَمْدُ لله رَبِّ الْعَالَمِيْنَ.

Allāhumma ṣalli wa sallim wa bārik ʿalā Sayyīdinā wa Mawlanā Muḥammadin shajarati 'l-aṣli 'n-nūrānīyyati wa lamʿati 'l-qabḍati 'r-raḥmānīyyati wa afḍali 'l-khalīqati 'l-insānīyyati wa ashrafi 'ṣ-ṣūrati 'l-jismānīyyati wa maʿdini 'l-asrāri 'r-rabbānīyyati wa khazā'ini 'l-ʿulūmi 'l-iṣṭifā'īyyati, ṣāḥibi 'l-qabḍati 'l-aṣlīyyati wa 'l bahjati 's-sanīyyati wa 'r-rutbati 'l-ʿalīyyati, man indarajati 'n-nabīyyūna taḥta liwā'ihi fahum minhu wa ilayhi wa ṣalli wa sallim wa bārik ʿalayhi wa ʿalā ālihi wa ṣaḥbihi ʿadada mā khalaqta wa razaqta wa amatta wa aḥyayta ilā yawmi tabʿathu man afnayta wa sallim taslīman kathīra wa 'l-ḥamdulillāhi rabbi 'l-ʿalamīn.

O Allāh! Exalt, greet and bless our Master Muḥammad, the Tree of Original Light, the Sparkle of the Handful of Divine Mercy, the Best of All Humankind, the Noblest of Physical Frames, the Vessel of the Lord's Secrets and Storehouse of the Sciences of the Elect, the Possessor of the Original Divine Grasp, Resplendent Grace, and Uppermost Rank, under whose flag line up all the Prophets, so that they are from him and point to him. Bless, greet and sanctify him and his Family and Companions, to the number of all that You have ever created, sustained, caused to die, and caused to live again, to the Day You resurrect those You reduced to dust, and greet him with an abundant and endless greeting. Glory and praise belong to Allāh, the Lord of the Worlds!

2) Ṣalāt al-Fāṭiḥ, Salutation of the Victor ﷺ

(Read at least 1 time daily or 10 times after *ʿIshā*)

Scholars mentioned that if you recite this *ṣalawāt* one time, it will be as if you have recited *Dalā'il al-Khayrāt* 600,000 times. The value of this *ṣalawāt* is greater than if you were to make *ṣalawāt* on the number of human beings from the time of Sayyīdinā Adam عليه السلام until the Day of Judgment. If you have a problem, every night after *ʿIshā* make *wudu* and pray two *rakaʿats*, then ask Allāh ﷻ for an opening, reciting *Ṣalāt al-Fāṭiḥ* up to ten times, which is the *ṣalāt* of The Opener that Opens Everything ﷻ! Continue reciting and don't say, "I'm fed up and won't ask anymore," as you will also be rewarded for your patience.

اللَّهُمَّ صَلِّ عَلَى سَيِّدِنَا مُحَمَّدٍ الفَاتِحِ لِمَا أُغْلِقَ و الخَاتِمِ لِمَا سَبَقَ نَاصِرِ الحَقِّ بَالحَقِّ و الهَادِي إلى.صِرَاطِكَ المُسْتَقِيمِ و عَلَى آلِهِ حَقَّ قَدْرِهِ و مِقْدَارِهِ العَظِيم

Allāhumma ṣalli ʿalā Sayyīdinā Muḥammadini 'l-Fāṭiḥi limā ughliqa wa 'l-khātimi limā sabaq, nāṣiri 'l-ḥaqqi bi 'l-ḥaqqa wa 'l-hādī ilā ṣirāṭika 'l-mustaqīmi wa ʿalā ālihi ḥaqqa qadrihi wa miqdārihi 'l-ʿaẓīm.

O Allāh! Bless our Master Muḥammad who opened what was closed and who sealed what had gone before; he makes the truth victorious by the truth and he is the guide to Your Straight Path, and bless his Household as it befits his immense stature and splendor.

3) Ṣalāt al-Munajīyyah / Ṣalāt Tunjīnā, Salutation of Rescue (Read 10 times daily, recommended by Mawlana Shaykh Nazim)

اَللَّهُمَّ صَلِّ عَلَى سَيِّدِنَا مُحَمَّدٍ صَلاَةً تُنْجِينَا بِهَا مِنْ جَمِيعِ اْلاَحْوَالِ وَاْلآفَاتِ وَتَقْضِى لَنَا بِهَامِنْ جَمِيعَ الْحَاجَاتِ وَتُطَهِّرُنَا بِهَا مِنْ جَمِيعِ السَّيِّئَاتِ وَتَرْفَعُنَا بِهَا عِنْدَكَ اَعْلَى الدَّرَجَاتِ.وَتُبَلِّغُنَا بِهَا اَقْصَى الْغَايَاتِ مِنْ جَمِيعِ الْخُيْرَاتِ فِى الْحُيَاتِ وَبَعْدَ الْمُمَاتِ.

Allāhumma ṣalli ʿalā Sayyīdinā Muḥammadin ṣalātan tunjīnā bihā min jamīʿi 'l-aḥwāli wa 'l-āfāti wa taqḍī lanā bihā min jamīʿi 'l-ḥājāti wa tuṭahhirunā bihā min jamīʿi 's-sayyi'āti wa tarfaʿunā bihā ʿindaka ʿalā 'd-darajāti wa tuballighunā bihā aqṣā 'l-ghāyāt min jamīʿi 'l-khayrāti fi 'l-ḥayāt wa baʿd al-mamāt.

O Allāh! Exalt Muḥammad with blessings that deliver us from every fear, and by means of them fulfill our every need, and by means of them purify us from every sin, and by means of them raise us to the highest stations, and by means of them make us attain the furthest degrees in all that is good in this life and in the life after death.

4) Ṣalāt al-ʿĀlī al-Qadr, Salutation of Highest Value (For Claustrophobia) (Read 10 times after *ʿIshā* / 1 time on the night of *Jumūʿah*)

As mentioned by many *awlīyāullāh*, from the book, *"Sharḥ Ṣalawāt ad-Dardīr al-ʿAllāmah as-Sāwī"*, reciting this *ṣalawāt* will eliminate claustrophobia and bring ease to you in the grave. It will also remove the fear of the interrogating angels, *Munkar* and *Nakir*. Whoever recites this *ṣalawāt* once every Friday, upon his death the Prophet ﷺ will go with him to his burial and bury him with his own blessed hands!

Numerous *awlīyāullāh* have said, "Whoever recites this *ṣalawāt* even once on Friday or from Thursday evening onward, Allāh ﷻ will allow his soul to see the Exemplar of All Souls ﷺ," not only when his soul is leaving the body, but also when he is taken to the grave, until he sees the Prophet ﷺ is the one taking care of him in that grave. *Awlīyāullāh* say to be consistent in reading *as-Ṣalāt al-ʿĀlī al-Qadr* ten times daily and once on the night of *Jumuʿah,* which will bring you *khayr al-jasīm*, the uncountable good that comes from it. Also, the book *Fatḥ ar-Rasūl* states that who reads it ten times after ʿIshā will be rewarded as if they recited it all night.

اللَّهُمَّ صَلِّ وَسَلِّمْ وَبَارِكْ عَلَى سَيِّدِنَا مُحَمَّدٍ النَّبِيِّ الأُمِّيِّ الْحَبِيبِ الْعَالِي الْقَدْرِ الْعَظِيمِ الْجَاهِ وَعَلَى آلِهِ وَصَحْبِهِ وَسَلِّمْ

Allāhumma ṣalli ʿalā Sayyīdinā Muḥammadi ʾn-Nabīyyi ʾl-Umīyyi ʾl-Ḥabībi ʾl-ʿālīyyi ʾl-qadri ʾl-ʿaẓīmi ʾl-jāhi wa ʿalā ālihi wa ṣaḥbihi wa sallim.

O Allāh! Exalt and greet and bless our Master Muḥammad, the Unlettered Prophet, the Beloved of Highest Value, Possessing Immense Status, and on his Family ؓ and Companions ؓ and send them peace.

5) Ṣalawāt at-Taḥīyyāt, Salutation of the Prayer of Greeting (Read 1 time daily)

The Prophet ﷺ said that anyone who reads this *ṣalawāt* once daily will not feel the pangs of death and his soul will pass from this world smoothly, as the hadith mentions, "The soul of the *mu'min* will leave the body like a hair being pulled from ghee," so easily. Recite this *ṣalawāt* along with *Jawharat al-Kamāl* at least once daily.

السَّلَامُ عَلَيْكَ أَيُّهَا النَّبِيُّ وَرَحْمَةُ اللهِ وَبَرَكَاتُهُ

Aṣ-ṣalāmu ʿalayka ayyuha ʾn-nabīyyu wa raḥmatullāhi wa barakātuh.

O Prophet! Allāh's Peace, Blessings and Grace be upon you.

6) Jawharat al-Kamāl, Jewel of Perfection ﷺ (Read 7 times daily)

If you read this *ṣalawāt* seven times daily or more Sayyīdinā Muḥammad ﷺ will love you with a special love and you will not leave *dunyā* without becoming a *walī* of Allāh! By reciting this *ṣalawāt,* you are mentioning the highest names of the Prophet ﷺ, through which Allāh ﷻ will open for you what He has opened for His *Awlīyā.*

اللَّهُمَّ صَلِّ وَسَلِّمْ عَلَى عَيْنِ الرَّحْمَةِ الرَّبَّانِيَةِ وَاليَاقُوتَةِ الْمُتَحَقِّقَةِ الْحَائِطَةِ بِمَرْكَزِ الفُهُومِ والمَعَانِي،
وَنُورِ الأَكْوَانِ الْمُتَكَوِّنَةِ الآدَمِي صَاحِبِ الْحَقِّ الرَّبَّانِي، البَرْقِ الأَسْطَعِ بِمُزُونِ الأَرْبَاحِ المَالِئَةِ لِكُلِّ مُتَعَرِّضٍ مِنَ
البُحُورِ وَالأَوَانِي، وَنُورِكَ اللاَّمِعِ الذِي مَلأْتَ بِهِ كَوْنَكَ الْحَائِطِ بِأَمْكِنَةِ الْمَكَانِي،
اللَّهُمَّ صَلِّ وَسَلِّمْ عَلَى عَيْنِ الْحَقِّ التِي تَتَجَلَّى مِنْهَا عُرُوشُ الحَقَائِقِ عَيْنِ الْمَعَارِفِ الأَقْوَمِ صِرَاطِكَ التَّامِّ
الأَسْقَمِ، اللَّهُمَّ صَلِّ وَسَلِّمْ عَلَى طَلْعَةِ الْحَقِّ بِالْحَقِّ الكَنْزِ الأَعْظَمِ إِفَاضَتِكَ مِنْكَ إِلَيْكَ إِحَاطَةِ النُّورِ
الْمُطَلْسَمِ صَلَّى اللهُ عَلَيْهِ وَعَلَى آلِهِ، صَلاَةً تُعَرِّفُنَا بِهَا إِيَّاهُ

Allāhumma ṣalli wa sallim ʿalā ʿayni ʾr-raḥmati ʾr-rabbānīyyati wa ʾl-yāqūtati ʾl-mutaḥaqqiqati ʾl-ḥāʾiṭati bi-markazi ʾl-fuhūmi wa ʾl-maʿānī. Wa nūri ʾl-akwāni ʾl-mutakawwinati ʾl-ādamīyy ṣāḥibi ʾl-ḥaqqi ʾr-rabbānī. Al-barqi ʾl-asṭaʿi bi-muzūni ʾl-arbāḥi ʾl-māʾilati li-kulli mutaʿarriḍi mina ʾl-buḥūri wa ʾl-awānīyy. Wa nūrika ʾLlāmiʿi ʾLladhī malāʾta bihi kawnaka ʾl-ḥāʾiṭi bi-amkinati ʾl-makānī.

Allāhumma ṣalli wa sallim ʿalā ʿayni ʾl-ḥaqqi ʾLlatī tatajallā minhā ʿurūshu ʾl-ḥaqāiqi ʿayni ʾl-maʿārifi ʾl-aqwamu ṣirāṭika ʾt-tāmmi ʾl-asqam. Allāhumma ṣalli wa sallim ʿalā ṭalʿati ʾl-ḥaqqi bi ʾl-ḥaqqi ʾl-kanzi ʾl-āʿẓami ifāḍatika minka ilayka iḥāṭati ʾn-nūri ʾl-muṭalsam. SallAllāhu ʿalayhi wa ʿalā ālihi ṣalātan tuʿarrifunā bihā iyyāh.

O Allāh! Exalt and salute the Source of Divine Mercy, the True Ruby which Encompasses the Center of Comprehension and Meanings, the Light of the World, which is in fact the Son of Adam, the Possessor of Divine Truth, the Most-Luminous Lightning in the profitable rain clouds which fill all the intervening seas as receptacles, and the Bright Light with which You filled the universe and which surrounds the places of existence!

O Allāh! Bless and salute the Source of Truth from which manifestations of realities are manifest, the Source of Knowledge, the Most-Upright, the Complete and Most-Straight Path! O Allāh! Bless and salute the Advent of the Truth by the Truth, the Greatest Treasure, Your Overflowing that is coming from Itself to Itself, and the Circle of Mysterious Light! May Allāh bless the Prophet ﷺ and his Household ﷺ, a prayer that brings us to knowledge of him!

7) Ṣalawāt Ūli 'l-ʿAzam, Salutation of Prophets Possessing Highest Purpose (Read 3 times daily)

Reciting this *ṣalawāt* three times is equal to reading the entire *Dalā'il al-Khayrāt*.

اللّٰهُمَّ صَلِّ عَلَى سَيِّدِنَا مُحَمَّدٍ وَسَيِّدِنَا آدَمَ وَسَيِّدِنَا نُوحٍ وَسَيِّدِنَا إِبْرَاهِيمَ وَسَيِّدِنَا مُوسَى وَسَيِّدِنَا عِيسَى وَمَا بَيْنَهُمْ مِن النَّبِيِّينَ وَالْمُرْسَلِينَ صَلَوَاتُ اللهِ وَسَلَامُهُ عَلَيْهِمْ أَجْمَعِينَ.

Allāhumma ṣalli ʿalā Sayyīdinā Muḥammadin wa Sayyīdinā Ādama wa Sayyīdinā Nūḥin wa Sayyīdinā Ibrāhīma wa Sayyīdinā Mūsā wa Sayyīdinā ʿIsā wa mā baynahum mina 'n-nabīyyīna wa 'l-mursalīna ṣalawātu 'Llāhi wa salāmuhu ʿalayhim ajmaʿīn.

O Allāh exalt our masters Muḥammad, and Adam and Abraham, and Moses and Jesus and all the Prophets and Messengers between them, may the prayers and peace of Allāh be upon all of them!

8) Grandshaykh ʿAbdAllāh's Ṣalawāt (Read 100 times daily)

Grandshaykh ق said that if you are unable to recite *Dalā'il al-Khayrāt* as part of your daily *wird*, recite this *ṣalawāt* 100 times, which is the easiest and simplest form of *ṣalawāt* on the Prophet ﷺ, as it shows the humility of the Prophet ﷺ towards His Lord. That is why it is important to read *Dalā'il al-Khayrāt*, but if you cannot, then recite this *Ṣalāt* 100 times, which is commensurate to reading one daily chapter of *Dalā'il al-Khayrāt*, and advice to all of us from Grandshaykh ق:

> O my son/daughter, beloved one! In order to reach safety and win the Guidance of Allāh ﷻ, I have compiled for you the treasures of *ṣalawāt* on Prophet ﷺ. Keep them and don't lose them, so that with the *barakah* of *ṣalāt ʿalā an-Nabi* ﷺ and with the best of salutations, O my son, be careful not to lose the *ṣalāt* on the Prophet ﷺ as we are losing it a lot! Beware of letting it down, for the *ṣalāt* on the Prophet ﷺ is so very beneficial and so highly appreciated by the Divine Presence, and it is the Way and the Door of Perfection, and it is the Greatest Entrance! O my son! I advise you to keep them and perhaps you will meet with Prophet ﷺ either in a dream or by vision in the waking state.

اَللّٰهُمَّ صَلِّ عَلَى مُحَمَّدٍ وَعَلَى آلِ مُحَمَّدٍ وسَلِّم

Allāhumma ṣalli ʿalā Muḥammadin wa ʿalā āli Muḥammadin wa sallim.

O Allāh! Send blessings and peace upon Muḥammad ﷺ and the Family of Muḥammad ﷺ.

9) Ṣalawāt al-Askandarī (Read 10 times daily)

One day Jamāluddīn bin ʿAlī Askandarī ⬥ saw the Prophet ﷺ in a dream, who said, "Yā Muḥammad Ibn ʿAlī Askandarī! I will teach you some words that if you read them ten times, it will be as if you read your entire *wird* (spiritual devotions) all day and night with all its rewards. Repeat after me," and we are saying it now after the Prophet ﷺ:

اللَّهُمَّ صَلِّ عَلَى سَيِّدِنَا مُحَمَّدٍ السَّابِقِ لِلْخَلْقِ نُورُهُ وَرَحْمَةً لِلْعَالَمِينَ ظُهُورُهُ عَدَدَ مَنْ مَضَى مِنْ خَلْقِكَ وَمَنْ بَقِيَ وَمَنْ سَعِدَ مِنْهُم وَمَنْ شَقِيَ صَلَاةً تَسْتَغْرِقُ الْعَدَّ وَتُحِيطُ بِالْحَدِّ صَلَاةً لَا غَايَةَ لَهَا وَلَا إِنْتِهَاءَ ولَا أَمَدَ لَهَا وَلَا انْقِضَاءَ صَلَاةً دَائِمَةً بِدَوَامِكَ بَاقِيَةً بِبَقَائِكَ وَعَلَى آلِهِ وَصَحْبِهِ وَسَلِّمْ تَسْلِيمًا مِثْلَ ذَلِكَ.

اللَّهُمَّ صَلِّ عَلَى مُحَمَّدٍ وَعَلَى آلِ مُحَمَّدٍ وَاجْزِ مُحَمَّداً عَنَّا مَا هُوَ أَهْلُهُ اللَّهُمَّ صَلِّ عَلَى مُحَمَّدٍ وَعَلَى آلِ مُحَمَّدٍ عَدَدَ مَا عَلِمْتَ وَزِنَةَ مَا عَلِمْتَ وَمِلْءَ مَا عَلِمْتَ اللَّهُمَّ صَلِّ وَ سَلِّم وَ بَارِك عَلَى سَيِّدِنَا وَ مَوْلاَنَا مُحَمَّدٍ وَ عَلَى كُلِّ نَبِيٍ وَ عَلَى جِبْرِيلَ وَ عَلَى كُلِّ مَلَكٍ وَ عَلَى أَبِي بَكْرٍ وَ عَلَى كُلِّ وَلِيٍ.

Allāhumma ṣalli ʿalā Sayyīdinā Muḥammadini 'ṣ-ṣābiqi li 'l-khalqi nūruhu wa 'r-raḥmatan li 'l-ʿālamīna ẓuhūruhu ʿadada man madā min khalqika wa man baqīya wa man saʿida minhum wa man shaqīya ṣalātan tastaghriqu 'l-ʿadda wa tuḥītu bi 'l-ḥaddi ṣalātan lā ghāyata lahā wa lā 'ntihā wa lā amada lahā wa lā 'nqiḍā ṣalātan dāʾimatan bi-dawāmika bāqīyatan bi-baqāʾika wa ʿalā ālihi wa ṣaḥbihi wa sallim taslīman mithla dhālik.

Allāhumma ṣalli ʿalā Muḥammadin wa ʿalā āli Muḥammadin w'ajzi Muḥammadan ʿanna mā huwa ahluhu. Allāhumma ṣalli ʿalā Muḥammadin wa ʿalā āli Muḥammadin ʿadada mā ʿalimta wa zinata mā ʿalimta wa milʾā mā ʿalimta. Allāhumma ṣalli wa sallim wa bārik ʿalā Sayyīdinā wa Mawlānā Muḥammadin wa ʿalā kulli nabīyyin wa ʿalā Jibrāʾīla wa ʿalā kulli malakin wa ʿalā Abī Bakrin wa ʿalā kulli walīyyin.

O Allāh! Exalt our Master Muḥammad, whose light preceded all Creation, whose appearance is Mercy to All the Worlds, on the number of Your Creations that have passed before and the number of those that remain, those who are fortunate and those who are not, with blessings that exceed all count and that encompass all limits, blessings with no limits, no boundaries, ceaseless blessings that are eternal, enduring as You endure! And likewise bless his Family ⬥ and his Companions ⬥, and grant him and them abundant peace in like measure.

O Allāh, O my Lord! Exalt our Master Muḥammad and the Family of Muḥammad, and reward our Master Muḥammad just as he deserves to be rewarded. O Allāh! Exalt Muḥammad and the Family of Muḥammad on the number of Your Decorations and on the beauty of Your Decorations and as full as what You know. O Allāh, O my Lord! Exalt and greet and bless our Master Muḥammad and every Prophet, Jibrīl and every angel, Abū Bakr and every saint.

10) Ṣalawāt al-Bakrī

In the book *Kunūz al-Asrār,* page 30, it is mentioned that this *ṣalawāt* is equal to 100,000 *ṣalawāt.*

اللَّهُمَّ صَلِّ عَلَى سَيِّدِنَا مُحَمَّدٍ وَعَلَى آلِهِ صَلَاةً تَزِنُ الأَرْضِينَ وَالسَّمَوَاتِ عَدَدَ مَا فِي عِلْمِكَ عَدَدَ جَوَاهِرِ أَفْرَادِ كُرَةِ العَالَمِ
وَأَضْعَافَ ذَلِكَ إِنَّكَ حَمِيدٌ مَجِيد

Allāhumma ṣalli ʿalā Sayyīdinā Muḥammadin wa ʿalā ālihi ṣalātan tazina ʾl-arḍīna wa ʾs-samawāti ʿadada mā fī ʿilmika ʿadada jawāhiri afrādi kurrati ʾl-ʿālam wa aḍʿāfa dhālika innaka ḥamīdun majīd.

O Allāh! Send upon Sayyīdinā Muḥammad and his Family prayers as the weight of the earths and the skies, and all that is in Your Knowledge on the number of the jewels of the inhabitants of the universe and double that, for You are Praiseworthy and Glorious!

11) Ṣalawāt that Equals 100,000 Ṣalawāt (Read 1 time daily)

اللَّهُمَّ صَلِّ عَلَى سَيِّدِنَا مُحَمَّدٍ عَبْدِكَ وَنَبِيِّكَ وَرَسُولِكَ النَّبِيِّ الأُمِّيِّ وَعَلَى آلِهِ وَصَحْبِهِ وَسَلِّمْ تَسْلِيماً.بِقَدْرِ عَظَمَةِ ذَاتِكَ فِي
كُلِّ وَقْتٍ وَحِين

Allāhumma ṣalli ʿalā Sayyīdinā Muḥammadin ʿabdika wa nabīyyika wa rasūlika an-nabīyyi ʾl-ummīyy wa ʿalā ālihi wa ṣaḥbihi wa sallim taslīman bi qadari ʿazhamati dhātika fī kulli waqtin wa ḥīn.

O Allāh! Send prayers upon Sayyīdinā Muḥammad, Your Servant and Your Prophet and Your Messenger, the Unlettered Prophet, and send peace and greetings as plenty as the Magnificence of Your Essence, in all times and moments.

12) Ṣalāt al-Kāmil, The Prayer upon the Perfect One ﷺ

(Read 1 time daily between *Maghrib* and *ʿIshā*)

This is the most honored *ṣalawāt* about which *awlīyāullāh* said one recitation equals 70,000 *ṣalawāt*. In the Shafiʿī School they say it is rewarded without end, as Allāh's Perfection has no end! It is read between Maghrib and ʿIshā, especially to remove forgetfulness and to strengthen memory.

اَللَّهُمَّ صَلِّ وَسَلِّمْ وَبَارِكْ عَلَى سَيِّدِنَا مُحَمَّدٍ وَعَلَى آلِهِ كَمَا لَا نِهَايَةَ لِكَمَالِكَ وَعَدَدَ كَمَالِه

Allāhumma ṣalli wa sallim wa bārik 'alā Sayyīdinā Muḥammadin wa 'alā ālihi kamā lā nihāyata li-kamālika wa 'adada kamālih.

O Allāh! Bestow Your Blessings, Peace and Grace upon our Master Muḥammad and His Family without end just as there is no end to Your Perfection and on the number of perfections with which You dressed him!

13) Ṣalawāt Kamālīya, The Praise of Perfection

Ṣalawāt Kamālīya is similar to *Aṣ-Ṣalāt al-Kāmil,* but with the difference of adding *'adada kamālillāh wa kamā yalīqu bi kamālihi,* "on the number of Allāh's Perfection and on the greatness of the word 'perfection' itself," which is not what we understand, but rather Divine Perfection that has no less or no more, the highest level of Divine Uncreated Perfection! In some narrations that are more commonly followed in the Shāfi'ī School and in Middle Eastern countries, it is said there is no end to the reward for this *salawāt,* and therefore, it cannot be said to be equal only to 600,000 or 1,000,000 *ṣalāt* as it has no end in reward and benefit, just as Allāh's Perfection has no end!

اللَّهُمَّ صَلِّ وَبَارِكَ عَلَى سَيِّدِنَا مُحَمَّدٍ وَعَلَى آلِهِ عَدَدَ كَمَالِ الله وَكَمَا يَلِيقُ بِكَمَالِهِ

Allāhumma salli wa bārik 'alā Sayyīdinā Muḥammadin wa 'alā ālihi 'adada kamālillāh wa kamā yalīqu bi kamālihi.

O Allāh! Bestow Your Blessings, Peace and Grace upon our Master Muḥammad and upon his Family according to the Perfection of Allāh ﷻ and as befits his perfection!

14) Ṣalāt as-Sa'adah, Praises of Happiness

(Read 1 time or 70 times daily)

In the book *Afḍal as-Ṣalawāt* by Shaykh Aḥmad as-Sāwī, it is said that if you read this *ṣalawāt* once, it is rewarded as if you have made *ṣalawāt* 600,000 times, and if you recite it 70 times daily, you will be released from Hellfire.

اللَّهُمَّ صَلِّ عَلَى سَيِّدِنَا مُحَمَّدٍ عَدَدَ مَا فِي عِلْمِ اللهِ صَلاَةً دَائِمَةً بِدَوَامِ مُلْكِ الله.

Allāhumma ṣalli 'alā Sayyīdinā wa Mawlanā Muḥammadin 'adada mā fī 'ilmillāhi ṣalātan dā'imatan bi-dawāmi mulkillāh.

O Allāh! Exalt and send peace on our Leader and Master Muḥammad on the number of what exists in Allāh's Knowledge with ongoing prayers as long as Allāh's Kingdom exists.

15) Ṣalawāt adh-Dhātīyyah, Prayer of The Essence
(Read 1 time daily)

Ṣalawāt adh-Dhātīyyah uses uncommon Arabic language. Sayyīdinā Muḥyuddīn ibn ʿArabi ق compiled it and it has so many deep, hidden meanings! This *ṣalawāt* was found in the *masjid* of al-Azhar University in Egypt and also appears in older copies of *Dalā'il al-Khayrāt.* One recitation of this *ṣalawāt* will bring you countless *barakah,* as if you are reciting *Dalā'il al-Khayrāt* all day every day, and you will get 70,000 rewards and blessings!

اللَّهُمَّ صَلِّ عَلَى الذَّاتِ الْمُطَلْسَمِ وَالْغَيْبِ الْمُطَمْطَمِ لاَهُوتِ الْجَمَالِ نَاسُوتِ الْوِصَالِ طَلْعَةِ الْحَقِّ كَنْزِ عَيْنِ إِنْسَانِ الْأَزَلِ فِي نَشْرِ مَنْ لَمْ يَزَلْ فِي قَابَ نَاسُوتِ الْوِصَالِ الْأَقْرَبْ اللَّهُمَّ صَلِّ بِهِ مِنْهُ فِيهِ عَلَيْهِ وَسَلَّمْ.

Allāhumma ṣalli ʿalā ʿdh-dhāti ʾl-muṭalsami wa ʾl-ghaybi ʾl-muṭamṭami lāhūti ʾl-jamāli nāsūti ʾl-wiṣāli ṭalʿati ʾl-ḥaqqi kanzi ʿayni insāni ʾl-azali fī nashri man lam yazal fī qāba nāsūti ʾl-wiṣāli ʾl-aqrab. Allāhumma ṣalli bihi minhu fīhi ʿalayhi wa sallam.

Here Allāh ﷻ sends His Prayers and Praises on the Essence of Prophet ﷺ, about which no one knows as it is hidden and one cannot penetrate its realities without knowing the secret codes needed to open and decode them.

Adh-dhāti 'l-Muṭalsam, "the Covered Essence that no one can open." *Al-Ghaybi 'l-Muṭamṭam,* "the Absolute Unseen that no one can reach or discuss." *Lāhūt al-Jamāl,* there is no one more beautiful than Prophet ﷺ; he is "the Beauty of this Universe and the Heavens!" *"Lāhūt"* means "that which belongs to earth" and *"Nāsūt"* is the connection from earth to heavens, which is Sayyīdinā Muḥammad ﷺ.

Ṭalʿati 'l-Ḥaqq, "the Appearance of Truth, where Allāh ﷻ dressed him with the dresses of Justice and Beauty!"

Insāni 'l-azali fi nashri man lam yazal, "He is the human being coming from the One Who is from *Azal,* pre-eternity, to *Abad,* eternity, who will open from the secrets of Heavenly Beautiful Names and Attributes."

Fī qāba nāsūti 'l-wiṣāli 'l-aqrab, "He opens only to those who reached the connection between the Earthly and Heavenly life, to whom he opens as they move forward to Heavens."

Ṣalli bihi (different than "*ṣalli ʿalayh*") means, "Make the *ṣalāt* through the Prophet ﷺ, *minhu,* 'from him to him', *fīhi,* 'in him', and *ʿalayhi,* 'upon him'!"

16) Variation of Ṣalawāt al-Askandarī (Read 1 time daily)

If you read this one time, Allāh ﷻ will waive 100,000 sins! With only one recitation of this *ṣalawāt* Allāh ﷻ will forgive and take away 100,000 grave sins, *kabā'ir;* with two recitations, 200,000 grave sins; with three recitations, 300,000 grave sins; and with ten recitations, one-million grave sins!

اللّهُمَ صَلِّ عَلَى سَيِّدِنَا مُحَمَّدٍ السَّابِقِ لِلْخَلْقِ نُوْرُهُ، وَالرَّحْمَةِ لِلْعَالَمِيْنَ ظُهُوْرُهُ، عَدَدَ مَنْ مَضَىْ مِنْ خَلْقِكَ وَمَنْ بَقِيَ، وَمَنْ سَعِدَ مِنْهُمْ وَمَنْ شَقِيَ، صَلَاةً تَسْتَغْرِقُ الْعَدَّ، وَتُحِيْطُ بِالْحَدِّ، صَلَاةً لَا غَايَةَ لَهَا وَلَا مُنْتَهَى وَلَا إِنْقِضَا، وَتُنِيْلُنَا بِهَا مِنْكَ الرِّضَا، صَلَاةً دَائِمَةً بِدَوَامِكَ وَبَاقِيَةٌ بِبَقَائِكَ الَىَّ.يَوْمِ الْدِّيْنِ، وَعَلَىَ آلِهِ وَصَحْبِهِ وَسَلِّمْ مِثْلَ ذَلِكَ

Allāhumma ṣalli 'alā Sayyīdinā Muḥammadini 's-sābiqi li 'l-khalqi nūruhu wa 'r-raḥmati li 'l-'ālamīna ẓuhūruhu 'adada man maḍā min khalqika wa man baqīya wa man sa'ida minhum wa man sḥaqīya ṣalātan tastaghriqu 'l-'adda wa tuḥītu bi 'l-ḥaddi ṣalātan lā ghāyata lahā wa lā muntahā wa lā 'nqiḍā wa tunīlanā bihā minka 'r-riḍā ṣalātan dā'imatan bi-dawāmika bāqīyatun bi-baqāika ilā yawmi 'd-dīni wa 'alā ālihi wa ṣāḥbihi wa sallim mithla dhālik.

O Allāh! Exalt our Master Muḥammad, whose Light preceded all Creation, whose appearance is Mercy to All the Worlds, on the number of Your Creations which have passed before and the number of those which remain, those who are fortunate and those who are not, with blessings which exceed all count and which encompass all limits, blessings with no limits, no boundaries, through which You grant us Your Good Pleasure, ceaseless blessings which are eternal, enduring as You endure.

O Allāh! Bless our Master Muḥammad ﷺ, whose heart is so full with Your Glory, and whose eyes are so full of Your Beauty that he came to be overjoyed, supported and victorious! And likewise, bless his Family and Companions, and grant him and them abundant peace, and praise be to Allāh ﷻ for all of that. (*Dalā'il al-Khayrāt*)

17) Sayyid aṣ-Ṣalawāt, The Master of Salutations upon the Prophet ﷺ

As an addition to Sayyīdinā ʿAlī's *Ṣalawāt*, this was given by the Prophet ﷺ in a vision of Shaykh Sharafuddin ق, who said, "Reciting this *ṣalawāt* even once in your lifetime is heavier than if all Creation stood 24 hours in *ṣalawāt*, repeating it all their lives, and this *ṣalawāt* will be heavier on the Scale than all of their *ṣalawāt* combined. Also, if you recite this *ṣalawāt* in front of the *Muwājaha al-Sharifah* (Gate to the Prophet's Noble Grave) in *Madīnatu 'l-Munawwara*, not only will you be granted the *ṣalawāt* of all Creation, but you will be rewarded directly by Allāh ﷻ, and there is no way of knowing how much Allāh ﷻ rewards for this *ṣalawāt*."

عَلَى أَشْرَفِ العَالَمِينَ سَيِّدِنا مُحَمَّدٍ الصَّلَوَاتْ
عَلَى أَفْضَلِ العَالَمِينَ سَيِّدِنا مُحَمَّدٍ الصَّلَوَاتْ
عَلَى أَكْمَلِ العَالَمِينَ سَيِّدِنا مُحَمَّدٍ الصَّلَوَاتْ

صَلَوَاتُ اللهِ تَعَالَى وَمَلَائِكَتِهِ وَأَنْبِيَائِهِ وَرُسُلِهِ وَجَمِيعِ خَلْقِهِ عَلَى مُحَمَّدٍ وَعَلَى آلِ مُحَمَّدٍ، عَلَيهِ وَعَلَيهِمُ السَّلَامُ وَرَحْمَةُ اللهِ
تَعَالَى وَبَرَكَاتُهُ وَرَضِيَ اللهُ تَبَارَكَ وَتَعَالَى عَنْ سَادَاتِنَا أَصْحَابِ رَسُولِ اللهِ أَجْمَعِين وَعَنِ التَّابِعِينَ بِهِمْ بِإِحْسَانٍ وَعَنِ
الأَئِمَّةِ المُجْتَهِدِينَ المَاضِينَ وَعَنِ العُلَمَاءِ المُتَّقِينَ وَعَنِ الأَوْلِيَاءِ الصَّالِحِينَ وَعَنْ مَشَايِخِنَا فِي الطَّرِيقَةِ النَّقْشْبَنْدِيَّةِ العَلِيَّةِ،
قَدَّسَ اللهُ تَعَالَى أَرْوَاحَهُمُ الزَّكِيَّةَ وَنَوَّرَ اللهُ تَعَالَى أَضْرِحَتَهُمُ المُبَارَكَةَ وَأَعَادَ اللهُ تَعَالَى عَلَيْنَا مِنْ بَرَكَاتِهِمْ وَفُيُوضَاتِهِمْ دَائِمًا
وَالحَمْدُ للهِ رَبِّ العَالَمِينَ - الفَاتِحَة

ʿAlā ashrafi 'l-ʿālamīna Sayyīdinā Muḥammadini 'ṣ-ṣalawāt.
ʿAlā afḍali 'l-ʿālamīna Sayyīdinā Muḥammadini 'ṣ-ṣalawāt.
ʿAlā akmali 'l-ʿālamīna Sayyīdinā Muḥammadini 'ṣ-ṣalawāt.

Ṣalawātullāhi taʿālā wa malā'ikatihi wa anbīyāihi wa rusulihi wa jamīʿi khalqihi ʿalā Muḥammadin wa ʿalā āli Muḥammad ʿalayhi wa ʿalayhimu 's-salām wa raḥmatullāhi taʿālā wa barakātuh.

Wa raḍīy-Allāhu tabāraka wa taʿālā ʿan sādātinā aṣḥābi rasūlillāhi ajmaʿīn. Wa ʿani 't-tābiʿīna bihim bi-iḥsānin, wa ʿani 'l-a'immati 'l-mujtahidīni 'l-māḍīn, wa ʿani 'l-ʿulamāi 'l-muttaqīn, wa ʿani 'l-awlīyāi 'ṣ-ṣāliḥīn, wa ʿan mashāyikhinā fi 'ṭ-ṭarīqati 'n Naqshbandīyyati 'l-ʿalīyyah, qaddas-Allāhu taʿālā arwāḥahumu 'z-zakīyyat wa nawwar-Allāhu taʿālā aḍriḥatahumu 'l-mubārakah wa aʿād-Allāhū taʿālā ʿalaynā min barakātihim wa fuyūḍātihim dā'iman wa 'l-ḥamdulillāhi rabbi 'l-ʿālamīn. Al-Fātiḥah.

Upon the Noblest of all Creation, our Master Muḥammad, blessings!
Upon the Most Preferred of all Creation, our Master Muḥammad, blessings!
Upon the most Perfect of all Creation, our Master Muḥammad, blessings!

Blessings of Allāh Almighty, of His Angels, of His Prophets, of His Messengers, and all Creation be upon Muḥammad and the Family of Muḥammad; may the Peace and Mercy of Allāh Almighty and His Blessings be upon him and upon them.

May Allāh, the Blessed and Most High, be pleased with every one of our Masters, the Companions of the Emissary of God, and with those who followed them in excellence, and with the early masters of juristic reasoning, and with the pious scholars, and the righteous saints and with our Shaykhs in the exalted Naqshbandi Sufi Order. May Allāh Almighty sanctify their pure souls and illuminate their blessed graves. May Allāh Almighty always return to us of their blessings and overflowing bounty. All praise belongs to Allāh, the Lord of all the Worlds! Al-Fātiḥah.

18) Ṣalawāt of Sayyīdinā ʿAlī ﵁

(Read 3 times daily, 100 times on *Jumuʿah*)

Sayyīdinā ʿAlī ﵁ said, "If you read this *ṣalawāt* three times daily and a hundred times on *Jumūʿah*, it will be as if you have read the *ṣalawāt* of all Creation, including *ins* (humankind), *jinn*, angels, and anything that makes *ṣalawāt* on Sayyīdinā Muḥammad ﷺ, and the Prophet ﷺ will take you by the hand to Paradise." This *ṣalawāt* is the door to Sayyīdinā Muḥammad ﷺ, as it was given from Prophet ﷺ to Sayyīdinā ʿAlī ﵁

صَلَوَاتُ اللهِ تعالى ومَلائِكَتِهِ وأَنْبيائِهِ ورُسُلِهِ وَجميعِ خَلْقِهِ على مُحَمَّدٍ وعَلى آلِ مُحَمَّدٍ، علَيْه وعلَيْهِمُ السَّلامُ ورَحْمَةُ الله تَعالى وبَرَكاتُهُ.

Ṣalawātullāhi taʿālā wa malāʾikatihi wa anbīyāʾihi wa rusulihi wa jamiʿī khalqihi ʿalā Muḥammadin wa ʿalā āli Muḥammad ʿalayhi wa ʿalayhimu ʾṣ-ṣalām wa raḥmatullāhi taʿālā wa barakātuh.

Blessings of Allāh Almighty, of His Angels, of His Prophets, of His Messengers, and all Creation be upon Muḥammad and the Family of Muḥammad; may the Peace and Mercy of Allāh Almighty and His Blessings be upon him and upon them!

Recite on *Jumū ʿah*

1. Ṣalāt al-ʿĀlī al-Qadr, Salutation of Highest Value (For Claustrophobia)
1. Ṣalawāt of Sayyīdinā ʿAlī
2. Ṣalawāt To See Your Lord in a Dream

1) Ṣalāt al-ʿĀlī al-Qadr, Salutation of Highest Value (For Claustrophobia)

(Read 10 times after *ʿIshā*/1 time on the night of *Jumūʿah*)

As mentioned by many *awlīyāullāh*, from the book, *"Sharḥ Ṣalawāt ad-Dardīr al-ʿAllāmah as-Sāwī"*, reciting this *ṣalawāt* will eliminate claustrophobia and bring ease to you in the grave. It will also remove the fear of the interrogating angels, *Munkar* and *Nakir*. Whoever recites this *ṣalawāt* once every Friday, upon his death the Prophet ﷺ will go with him to his burial and bury him with his own blessed hands!

Numerous *awlīyāullāh* have said, "Whoever recites this *ṣalawāt* even once on Friday or from Thursday evening onward, Allāh ﷻ will allow his soul to see the Exemplar of All Souls ﷺ," not only when his soul is leaving the body, but also when he is taken to the grave, until he sees the Prophet ﷺ is the one taking care of him in that grave. *Awlīyāullāh* say to be consistent in reading *as-Ṣalāt al-ʿĀlī al-Qadr* ten times daily and once on the night of *Jumuʿah,* which will bring you *khayr al-jasīm*, the uncountable good that comes from it. Also, the book *Faṭḥ ar-Rasūl* states that who reads it ten times after ʿIshā will be rewarded as if they recited it all night.

اللَّهُمَّ صَلِّ وَسَلِّمْ وَبَارِكْ عَلَى سَيِّدِنَا مُحَمَّدٍ النَّبِيِّ الأُمِّيِّ الْحَبِيبِ الْعَالِي الْقَدْرِ الْعَظِيمِ الْجَاهِ وَعَلَى.آلِهِ وَصَحْبِهِ وَسَلِّمْ

Allāhumma ṣalli ʿalā Sayyīdinā Muḥammadi ʼn-Nabīyyi ʼl-Umīyyi ʼl-Ḥabībi ʼl-ʿālīyyi ʼl-qadri ʼl-ʿaẓīmi ʼl-jāhi wa ʿalā ālihi wa ṣaḥbihi wa sallim.

O Allāh! Exalt and greet and bless our Master Muḥammad, the Unlettered Prophet, the Beloved of Highest Value, Possessing Immense Status, and on his Family ﵃ and Companions ﵃ and send them peace.

2) Ṣalawāt of Sayyīdinā ʿAlī ﷛

(Read 3 times daily, 100 times on *Jumuʿah*)

Sayyīdinā ʿAlī ﷛ said, "If you read this *ṣalawāt* three times daily and a hundred times on *Jumuʿah,* it will be as if you have read the *ṣalawāt* of all Creation, including *ins, jinn,* angels, and anything that makes *ṣalawāt* on Sayyīdinā Muḥammad ﷺ, and the Prophet ﷺ will take you by the hand to Paradise."

صَلَوَاتُ اللهِ تعالى ومَلائِكَتِهِ وأنبيائه ورَسُلِهِ وجميعِ خَلْقِهِ على مُحَمِّدٍ وعلى آلِ مُحَمَّدٍ، عليه وعليهمُ السَّلامُ ورَحْمَةُ الله تَعالى وبرَكاتُهُ

Ṣalawātullāhi taʿālā wa malāʾikatihi wa anbīyāʾihi wa rusulihi wa jamiʿī khalqihi ʿalā Muḥammadin wa ʿalā āli Muḥammad ʿalayhi wa ʿalayhimu ʼṣ-ṣalām wa raḥmatullāhi taʿālā wa barakātuh.

Blessings of Allāh Almighty, of His Angels, of His Prophets, of His Messengers, and all Creation be upon Muḥammad and the Family of Muḥammad; may the Peace and Mercy of Allāh Almighty and His Blessings be upon him and upon them!

3) Ṣalawāt To See Your Lord in a Dream
(Read 1,000 times on *Jumu`ah*)

In *Kunūz al-Asrār,* page 30, it is said that whoever recites this *ṣalawāt* one-thousand times on *Jumuʿah* will see Allāh ﷻ in his dream, as the Prophet ﷺ said, "I saw my Lord coming to me smiling." *Inshā'Allāh,* Allāh ﷻ will grant that you see His Manifestations or His Prophet ﷺ, or your place in Paradise. If for any reason you did not see these, continue reciting it for five weeks, as it was tried and reciters were able to see!

Abū Faḍl Qawmānī (may Allāh have mercy on him) narrates that a person came to him from Khurāsān and said, "I was in Madīnat al-Munawwara. I saw the Noble Prophet ﷺ in my dream and he said to me, 'When you go to Hamdān, convey my salutations to Abū Faḍl Qawmānī.' I asked the reason for this. The Noble Prophet ﷺ said, 'He confers the following blessings upon me more than a hundred times daily.' Abū Fadl Qawmānī says, "This person swore that he neither knew me nor had he ever heard my name before the Noble Prophet ﷺ informed him in his dream. I tried to give him some food, but he refused, saying, 'I am not going to sell (take anything in exchange) for the message of the Noble Prophet ﷺ!' I never saw that person after this." (*Al-Qawl al-Badīʿ*)

اللَّهُمَّ صَلِّ عَلَى سَيِّدِنَا مُحَمَّد النَّبِيِّ الأُمِّيِّ جَزَى اللهُ عَنَّا مُحَمَّدً مَّا هُوَ اَهْلُه

Allāhumma ṣalli ʿalā Sayyīdinā Muḥammadi 'n-Nabīyyi 'l-Ummīyy jazā-Allāhu ʿannā Muḥammadan mā hūwa āhluh.

O Allāh! Bless our Master Muḥammad, the Unlettered Prophet. May Allāh reward Muḥammad ﷺ on our behalf, the benefits that he deserves.

Recite for Specific Benefit

1. Ṣalawāt to See Prophet ﷺ in a Dream
2. Ṣalawāt al-Shafaʿah, Salutation of Intercession and to See Prophet ﷺ in a Dream
3. Ṣalawāt for Shifā (Healing)
4. Ṣalawāt Īmām ash-Shāfiʿī

1) Ṣalawāt to See Prophet ﷺ in a Dream (Read 71 times)

To see the Prophet ﷺ, recite this 71 times and you will see him and smell his Holy Fragrance!

اللّٰهُمَّ صَلِّ عَلَى مُحَمَّدٍ وَعَلَى آلِ مُحَمَّدٍ كَمَا أَمَرْتَنَا أَنْ نُصَلِّيَ عَلَيه.

Allāhumma ṣalli ʿalā Muḥammadin wa ʿalā āli Muḥammadin kamā amartanā an nuṣallīya ʿalayh.

O Allāh! Exalt Muḥammad and the Family of Muḥammad as You ordered us to exalt him.

2) Ṣalawāt Shafaʿah, Salutation of Intercession and to See Prophet ﷺ in a Dream (Recite until you fall asleep)

Īmām Shaʿrānī related that the Prophet ﷺ said, "Who saw me in the dream really saw me, because Shaytan cannot assume my image. And whoever makes *ṣalawāt* in this way will see me in the dream, and who sees me in the dream will see me in the Day of Judgment, and whoever sees me in the Day of Judgment, I will intercede for him and whoever I intercede for will drink from my basin, the *Ḥawḍ al-Kawthar* in Paradise, and whoever drinks from *al-Kawthar* will be prohibited from entering Hellfire. "I said to myself, "I must recite this!" and I recited it before I slept, until I fell asleep. I looked at the moon and saw the Prophet's honorable face, and I spoke with him. Then *ghāba fi 'l-qamar*, I felt he was in the moon until he disappeared. I asked Allāh ﷻ that for the sake of this *ṣalawāt*, give me all the favors He gives, not the normal provisions, but the ones He gave to His Beloved One, Sayyīdinā Muḥammad ﷺ, that He promised to every *mu'min*, and I felt that I am getting it. (See "*Afḍal as-Ṣalawāt*", Page 58)

Look at the moon and close your eyes; you will feel like the Prophet's honorable face is there appearing and disappearing, as Īmām Shaʿrānī said. Recite this *ṣalawāt* and *inshā'Allāh* you will see the Prophet ﷺ.

اَللّٰهُمَّ صَلِّ عَلَى رُوحِ سَيِّدِنَا مُحَمَّدٍ فِي الْأَرْوَاحِ وَعَلَى جَسَدِهِ فِي الْأَجْسَادِ وَعَلَى قَبْرِهِ فِي الْقُبُوْرِ وَعَلَى الِهِ وَصَحْبِهِ وَسَلِّم.

Allāhumma ṣalli ʿalā rūḥi Sayyīdinā Muḥammadin fi 'l-arwāḥi wa ʿalā jasadihi fi 'l-ajsādi wa ʿalā qabrihi fi 'l-qubūri wa ʿalā ālihi wa ṣaḥbihi wa sallim.

O Allāh! Shower Your Blessings on the Soul of Muḥammad amongst all souls, on the Heart of Muḥammad amongst all hearts, and on the Body of Muḥammad amongst all bodies, and on the Grave of Muḥammad amongst all graves. (*Dalā'il al-Khayrāt*)

3) Ṣalawāt for Shifā (Healing) (Read 3 times at Fajr)

Through this *ṣalawāt*, as soon as we say, "O Allāh! Praise the Prophet ﷺ on the number of sicknesses and cures," Allāh ﷻ takes away all (spiritual and physical) illnesses from us and gives us the cure, as every illness has its cure. This *ṣalawāt* is to cure every spiritual illness from the 800 bad characteristics; you must make *ṣalawāt* on the Prophet ﷺ in this form before illnesses burst into new forms in your body. Reciting this *ṣalawāt* will take away all the rust from our hearts and give provision for the soul.

اللَّهُمَّ صَلِّ عَلَى سَيِّدِنَا مُحَمَّدٍ وَعَلَى آلِ سَيِّدِنَا مُحَمَّد بِعَدَدِ كُلِّ دَاءٍ وَ دواءٍ وَ بَارِك وَ سَلِّمْ عَليه.وَعَلَيهِمْ كَثِيرًا كثيرا وَالحَمْدُ لله رَبِّ العَالَمِيْنْ

Allāhumma ṣalli ʿalā Sayyīdinā Muḥammadin wa ʿalā āli Sayyīdinā Muḥammad bi ʿadadi kulli dā'in wa dawā'in wa bārik wa sallim ʿalayhi wa ʿalayhim kathīran kathīra, wa 'l-ḥamdulillāhi rabbi 'l-ʿālamīn.

O Allāh! Upon Muḥammad and the Family of Muḥammad be blessings, according to the number of every illness and cure. Bless and grant peace to him and them, many times, endlessly. And praise belongs to Allāh, Lord of the Worlds.

(From The Naqshbandi Awrad Book)

4) Ṣalawāt Imam ash-Shāfiʿī ﵁

ʿAbdAllāh al-Hakam (a great *ʿamīr* in the time of Īmām Shāfiʿī) said, "I saw Īmām ash-Shāfiʿī in my dream and asked him, 'What has Allāh done with you?' and he replied, 'He poured His Mercy on me, forgave me and decorated Paradise for me, which came to me as a bride adorned with all her ornaments for her husband! They showered me with angels and heavenly ornaments like they throw rose petals over the bride and groom in *dunyā*.' I asked him, 'How did you attain this level?' He said, 'Someone told me to recite a specific *ṣalawāt*, which I did.'"

Recite this *ṣalawāt* to enter Paradise without being questioned:

للّهُمَّ صَلِّ على محمد عدد ما ذكره الذاكرون وغفل عن ذكره الغافلون

Allāhumma salli ʿalā Muḥammadin ʿadada mā dhakarahu 'dh-dhākirūn wa ghafala ʿan dhikrihi 'l-ghāfilūn.

O Allāh! Send blessings upon Muḥammad as much as he is remembered by those who remember him, and send blessings upon Muḥammad as much as his remembrance is left by the heedless.

Lightning Source UK Ltd.
Milton Keynes UK
UKHW040342061118
331803UK00002B/401/P

9 781930 409910